Original title:
Houseplants in Harmony

Copyright © 2025 Creative Arts Management OÜ
All rights reserved.

Author: Nora Sinclair
ISBN HARDBACK: 978-1-80581-876-2
ISBN PAPERBACK: 978-1-80581-403-0
ISBN EBOOK: 978-1-80581-876-2

Verdant Whispers

In a pot, I find my friend,
A succulent's grin, it won't end.
We gossip about the light and shade,
While sipping dew, on perfectly laid.

Leafy Serenade

Oh, the spiky guy up on the shelf,
Complains to me, 'Why are you so stealth?'
I promise him that soon he'll shine,
Just needs a little sun with his wine.

Green Embrace

Cacti tell tales of desert nights,
While ferns dance under the lamp's bright lights.
Vines whisper secrets, tangled in a knot,
Of bugs and soil, we share quite a lot.

Blossoms in Unity

The flowers boast in colors bold,
Challenging the leaves to break the mold.
Together we giggle, we sway and spin,
In this fun little world, let the joy begin.

Living Tapestry

In a pot, a cactus grins,
While the fern sways, it spins.
'You prick, I'm soft!' the cacti tease,
A duo made of prickly ease.

The tomato blushed, forgot the stew,
While the basil munches, 'Is that my brew?'
Together they make a savory mess,
A garden party, I must confess!

The Dance of Petals

Tulips twirl in colors bright,
Bouncing blooms with pure delight.
'You think you're tall?' said the shy small moss,
'But I can dance; you're the boss!'

The daisies giggle, sway to the beat,
Waving to the sun, they're light on their feet.
'Let's throw a party for the bees!'
'But not too loud, or we'll scare the leaves!'

Roots Entwined

Roots underground, they twist and shout,
Whispering secrets, there's no doubt.
'You've got my toe!' said the eager sprout,
'We're tangled friends, there's fun throughout!'

Laughing in dirt, a muddy affair,
Gossiping bugs hover in the air.
'How's the light?' asked a shy old yarrow,
'Bright as my future, no need for sorrow!'

Canopy Conversations

Leaves above chatter with glee,
Branching out like a grand marquee.
'Shade or light, what's your game?'
'The cooler spot, I'm never the same!'

A monkey mask tosses some dirt,
While the orchids giggle in their flirty shirt.
'Let's throw in some sunlight and cheer!'
'Don't forget the rain; it's the best here!'

Sprouts of Community

In the pot, a party's brewing,
Pothos whispers, 'Keep it moving!'
Succulents sway to the funky beat,
While cacti dance with spiky feet.

The fern insists it's time to share,
Tales of growth beyond compare.
The peace lily sings a lullaby,
While little ferns just wave goodbye.

Radiance of Leaves

A spider plant spins a wild tale,
While philodendrons jump and flail.
Monstera hides, but wants a stage,
'Let's go viral!'—it's all the rage!

Sunshine filters through the green brigade,
Each leaf a note in the leafy parade.
The jade plant boasts, 'I'm rich in style!'
While snake plants smirk in green and guile.

Garden of Tranquility

In corners bright, the laughter grows,
As herbs conspire to tattle toes.
Lavender dreams of a spa retreat,
While basil's busy getting sweet.

Chill, said the thyme, and take a break,
Join in the fun, make no mistake!
With whispers low, they scheme all day,
To turn the drab to a bright bouquet.

Under the Verdant Canopy

Beneath the leaves, the gossip flows,
A rubber tree unveils its woes.
The bird of paradise strikes a pose,
While dracaena spreads its gossip prose.

In shade and warmth, they find their groove,
Each petal dancing, trying to prove.
The ficus claims the utmost charm,
While orchids swoon and turn on the charm.

Symphony of Sunshine

In a corner, a cactus sways,
Singing softly, brightening days.
The fern performs a leafy jig,
While the ivy hums, 'Look at me, I'm big!'

The spider plant starts a dance,
Inviting all to join the chance.
'Come on, pals, let's throw a bash,
With potting soil and a happy splash!'

Entwined in Nature's Breath

A pothos whispers slyly,
'Tell me, who's wearing that smile wryly?'
The peace lily rolls its eyes,
'Oh, it's just the drama, no surprise!'

As the snake plant stretches tall,
'Can you folks even hear my call?'
While the rubber tree, not done,
Says, 'You know I'm just having fun!'

Flourish and Thrive

In pots of wonder, stories bloom,
'Care for me, or I'll take up room!'
The bromeliad wears a party hat,
While the aloe grows a friendly spat.

Together they plot and scheme,
'Let's throw a feast; let's make it supreme!'
A banquet of water and tiny bugs,
'Who knew plant life could be so snug?'

Whispering Green Allies

The basil giggles, 'Is that a fly?'
The oregano joins, 'Oh my, oh my!'
Their garden pals nod with glee,
'Life's better when we're all carefree!'

Lettuce leads with a twisty spin,
'Who needs sunlight? Let's just grin!'
While thyme chimes in with a clever pun,
'In this green world, we're having fun!'

Nature's Tranquil Voice

In pots they sit, with smiles wide,
Leaves waving gently, side to side.
They gossip softly, plant to plant,
While roots do tango, grass and chant.

Sunshine beams, they drink in cheer,
Photosynthesis, their favorite beer.
A cactus cracks a prickly joke,
While ferns laugh loudly, never choke.

Essence of Eden

In the corner, a fern does sway,
With leafy limbs, it steals the day.
A spider plant spins tales so fine,
Of daring climbs and roots that twine.

The succulent winks, it's quite the tease,
Sipping sunlight with practiced ease.
A pothos plots its leafy schemes,
Dreams of vines and extravagant dreams.

Symphony of Sprouts

A chorus of greens, vibrant and bright,
Bouncing to rhythms of morning light.
A little moss hums a sleepy tune,
While the basil dances, bright as the moon.

The thyme sings softly, with notes so sweet,
Together they sway, a fragrant treat.
Restrictions? No! They grow and play,
Each leaf a note in a leafy ballet.

Verdant Balances

In quirky pots, they twist and sway,
Each leaf has something funny to say.
The ivy tickles the curious cat,
While the anthurium wears a fancy hat.

Laughter fills the room with glee,
As plants engage in their jubilee.
A playful riot of greens and gold,
In this wild kingdom, no one feels old.

The Lush Stereo

In the corner, ferns play jazz,
While succulents chill, sipping pizzazz.
Cacti provide the sharpest beats,
Together they sway, tapping their feet.

The pothos is the DJ today,
Spinning vines in a groovy way.
Umbrella trees do the cha-cha slide,
Who knew plants had so much pride?

String of hearts sings a love song,
But the peace lily hums all night long.
With every beat, they dance and spin,
Their leafy rhythm draws us in.

So join the party, don't be shy!
Grab some soil and reach for the sky.
In this lush stereo, fun never ends,
Where green dreams blossom and laughter blends.

Botanical Duet

A spider plant strums a tune,
While thyme joins with a gentle croon.
Their notes float soft on morning air,
A melody made without a care.

The jade plant hums a plucky beat,
As ferns flutter and sway on their feet.
Cacti play maracas with glee,
Who knew plants could rock out so free?

Orchids waltz in elegant style,
While peace lilies add that extra smile.
With every note, their leaves entwine,
Creating a duet that's simply divine.

So take a seat and take it in,
This botanical show is set to win.
With laughter and rhythm in full view,
In plant paradise, the fun's never through.

Verdant Affection

In a pot, love's tender embrace,
Where green leaves gather, a snug space.
Alocasia whispers sweet nothings,
While snake plants grumble about their things.

The pothos climbs, reaching for hugs,
While the bromeliad smiles and shrugs.
Once a shy bud, now a bold show,
Their leafy love is all aglow.

Sunflowers peek in, drifting close,
Their sunny charm, the plants engross.
With laughter blooming, they all unite,
In this verdant stage, everything's bright.

So gather round for this leafy affair,
With playful vibes dancing in the air.
The plants may be green, but don't you fret,
Their love-filled antics, you won't forget!

A Symphony of Growth

In the corner, leafy friends sway,
A cactus hums, oh what a display!
The dracaena dances, what a sight,
While the peace lily dreams of the night.

Pothos hangs out, swinging from a shelf,
Sipping on sunlight, oh bless its health!
The fern's waving fronds shout, 'Look at me!'
Joyous together, in perfect jubilee.

Tiny pots giggle, they never stop,
The spider plant's hairdo, a wild crop!
Its little babies cheer, 'We're a bunch!'
Plenty of green for a lively lunch.

A symphony plays, with soil and cheer,
Each leaf a note, music we hold dear!
Together they flourish, no room for gloom,
In this botanical, green-filled room.

Nurtured by Light

Sunlight pours in, a radiant feast,
All green friends gather, a perfect beast!
A little jade plant does a funny jig,
While succulents share jokes, oh what a gig!

The spider plant whispers, 'I need space!'
But the pothos, too curious, wants to race.
Light dances across their funny faces,
Growing together, in silly embraces.

The peace lily sighs, 'Water, please!'
While the snake plant simply sloughs off with ease.
In this cheerful plot, laughter has a say,
As they stretch for the sun, come what may.

Nurtured by rays, they giggle with glee,
Each leaf a chuckle, as bright as can be!
In this sunlit haven, it's all quite a show,
Harmony blooms, as we all know!

In the Company of Green

In the terracotta crew, they gossip and cheer,
Chlorophyll pals bring laughter near!
An aloe said, 'I've got all the spunk!'
While the fern rolled its eyes, 'What a hunk!'

The fiddle leaf fig strikes a pose so grand,
'Watch me, folks!' says the big leafy stand.
With each little breeze, they wiggle and sway,
In this company, they brighten the day.

A rubber tree boasts of its shiny flair,
While the philodendron twirls like it's fair!
In this garden giggle-fest, green is the theme,
With roots intertwined, they plot and they dream.

In the company of green, life's a delight,
Jokes exchanged, oh what a sight!
They thrive together, not a care in their leaf,
In this plant-filled joy, there's no room for grief.

Woven Ferns

Ferns weave tales in the softest of tones,
With whispered secrets and leafy drones.
In a patch of shade, they twirl and they spin,
Dancing together, like a whimsical kin.

Each frond has a story of joy or of woe,
Like a garden party, just put on a show!
The maidenhair blushes, the staghorn grins,
In this leafy party, fun surely begins.

They gossip and rustle, oh what a sound,
As bugs fly by, they all gather round.
With laughter like raindrops, they jive with the breeze,
In harmony woven, they do as they please.

So here's to the ferns, with their playful embrace,
In their gentle world, there's always a space!
For fun and for laughter, a leafy brigade,
Woven together, in sunshine and shade.

Ecstasy in Chlorophyll

In the corner, a fern does dance,
Swinging leaves in a leafy trance.
Cacti roll their prickly eyes,
While succulents giggle in disguise.

The pothos spills from shelf to floor,
As if it's trying to explore.
IV drip of sunshine, oh so bright,
Growing wild in pure delight.

Basil teases with fragrant chat,
While mint claims it's a wizard's hat.
"So magical," they all agree,
In their green laughter, wild and free.

But wait, here comes the great big bug,
A scary sight, a leafgreen thug!
The plants unite, a leafy squad,
To chase it out—oh, greeny applaud!

A Nest of Verdure

A spider plant swings like a kid,
With tendrils long, it won't stay hid.
The rubber tree with its glossy flair,
Announces, "I'm the coolest heir!"

Next door, the ivy's climbing high,
Said, "I'll reach the window, oh my!"
While peace lilies throw shade on foes,
Snickering softly as everyone grows.

They throw a party, a leafy bash,
With ferns and herbs making a splash.
Exotic tunes from the bamboo play,
While roots tap-dance in fine ballet.

But watch out for the mischief crew,
In perfect harmony, they break the dew!
With a swing of leaf and twist of vine,
This nest of green is simply divine!

Collective Joy in Photosynthesis

Chlorophyll giggles, sunlight beams,
Photosynthesis fuels wild dreams.
'Photosynthesiz-zzzz'—no one snores,
Plants partying while open doors!

The sage speaks in fragrant rhymes,
Telling tales of ancient times.
"Oh, leave it to me, I'll spice the stew!"
And thus, they chat while growing anew.

With every sip of morning sun,
Citrus trees join, "We're just having fun!"
As ferns flirt with the dappled light,
Loving life, oh what a sight!

And then a wiggle, a twist, a shake,
Bamboo stood up for goodness' sake!
"Let's toast our leaves, let's raise a cheer,
In our green world, we have no fear!

The Unity of Roots

In the soil where secrets lie,
Roots are swirling, oh my, oh my!
Tangled mess of friends galore,
Sharing whispers from the core.

A word of thanks from every sprout,
For nutrients flowing all about.
"Pass the water, and don't be shy!"
Yells the tomato, "You're the best, oh my!"

The wisdom speaks beneath the ground,
In unity, their joys abound.
"Let's grow together, hand in root!"
Mirthful laughter, such a hoot!

But oh dear vine, you've pulled my shoe,
In laughter, they all bid adieu.
With roots so thick and hearts so light,
Together they dance, a leafy flight!

Cradled by Green

In pots so snug, they sit so proud,
With leaves that wriggle, they dance aloud.
A cactus winks, a fern takes a dive,
Who knew plants could be so alive?

The peeking sun brings a daily laugh,
As succulents gossip, oh what a staff!
They whisper secrets, in silent cheer,
While my spider plant plays the chandelier!

A mischief of roots, a tango of stems,
Each tall green friend, a quirky gem.
With soil-stained hands, I join their tune,
As we all sway to the soft afternoon.

Together we thrive, quite the ensemble,
In their leafy lives, I can't help but ramble.
With pots of laughter and joy to share,
These green comedians, beyond compare!

Echoing Through the Foliage

In a leafy lodge, where whispers play,
There's a jade plant fretting, 'Will I grow today?'
A friendly orchid, blooms with a grin,
While in the corner, a rogue vine begins.

Ferns frown softly, in shades of green,
'Why do the humans keep us unseen?'
Yet underneath their breath, a chuckle slips,
As they watch my antics and tumbles and trips.

The begonias giggle, gossiping vines,
While pothos dangles, sharing punchlines.
A lopsided peace lily sighs with grace,
'At least I'm better than that dusty vase!'

Under the glow of a friendly light,
This botanical crew makes everything bright.
With laughter and quirks, they keep me in line,
In this green-tinged haven, we're all divine!

Flourishing in the Sun

Basking in sun, the plants all beam,
A rubber tree stretches, living the dream.
A sunflower points, with pride it shouts,
'Look at me, folks! I'm what life's about!'

The basil's a chef, with thoughts of stew,
While a petunia plays hide-and-seek too.
With shining leaves, they brace for a laugh,
Every leaf a hero in their green craft.

The little cacti, quite prickly and bold,
Share grand adventures of desert gold.
While back in the shade, the ferns throw a feast,
'Who invited the weeds? Now we're all deceased!'

In this garden stage, they frolic and play,
A comical cast, in their own green way.
With spontaneous joy, they give life a spin,
In their quirky kingdom, where laughter begins!

Nature's Collective Joy

In a leafy world, where laughter's supreme,
A fiddle-leaf fig has an ambitious dream.
While the succulents chuckle, in rows they align,
'Can we grow taller? It's part of the design!'

With vines all tangled, a plot to inspect,
A peppermint argues, 'We need more respect!'
A calathea rolls, with colorful flair,
As a dracaena shimmies without a care.

Together they make a delightful charade,
With sunny narrators, the jokes never fade.
Each petal and leaf, a punchline that glows,
As they share tales of their rooty woes.

In this riot of green, joy spirals high,
With hugs made of leaves and laughter nearby.
In nature's embrace, we twirl and enjoy,
As the giggles of green become our sweet joy!

A Living Palette

In pots of clay, they stand in cheer,
Each leaf a brush, vibrant and clear.
They gossip in whispers, under the light,
Determined to grow, with all of their might.

One cactus brags of its royal flair,
While the fern rolls eyes, and flips its hair.
A spider plant twirls, quite full of glee,
Planning a dance with the busy bee.

Oh, the antics of leaves, green and bright,
Playing tag in the warm sunlight.
They sing to the sun and giggle at rain,
In this wild, leafy world, joy is their gain.

So here's to the garden of chatter and cheer,
Where plants wear their quirks like a feathered spear.
With humor in growth, they flourish and thrive,
A wacky companionship, oh how they jive!

Whispered Secrets in Green

In a corner bright, the leaves conspire,
To share their secrets, never to tire.
A snake plant smirks, with a twist of its stem,
Plotting pranks on the poor little gem.

The succulents sip their morning brew,
Trading tales of the skies so blue.
"I bask all day, don't need much care,"
The aloe retorts, "That's simply not fair!"

"Remember when the sunbeam came shy?"
The pothos chimed, with a glint in its eye.
They laughed as the shadows danced on the ground,
Amid whispered joys, such treasures abound.

In this tapestry of life, green and grand,
Plants share their laughs, a merry band.
With hearts so light, and roots so deep,
In their leafy realm, joy's secrets they keep.

Flourishing Together

In a sunny spot, their laughter blooms,
Bright colors pop, dispelling the glooms.
The tradescantia flaunts its stripes,
While the ivy wiggles, plotting its gripes.

"Do you see the way the sunlight flows?"
Mused the peace lily, as it steals a pose.
The jade plant chuckled, "I'm rich as can be,
Rolling in coins and growing for free!"

They hold a summit at quarter-till two,
Arguing which one has the most dew.
With playful jabs and leaves in embrace,
Their bond shines bright in this green-filled space.

Here's to the power of friendship divine,
In verdant communities, all intertwine.
Through giggles and glee, they stretch for the sky,
Together they flourish, oh my, oh my!

Sacred Garden Conversations

In the garden's heart, the plants convene,
Sharing stories, a plant-powered scene.
A little green sprout, so eager to speak,
Tells of the rain, dripping down from its peak.

The fern rolls its fronds, puffing with pride,
"I'm the wisest here," it bumbled with stride.
While basil dreams of a flavorful feast,
"I'll spice up your lives, I'm the greenest beast!"

A calla lily twirls, so graceful and proud,
"Don't you wish you could dance, join the crowd?"
They'd break into laughter, rustling their leaves,
Finding joy in the light, such bliss none believe.

With each gentle sway, as sunlight warms,
These leafy companions embrace all their charms.
In playful discourse, they grow ever bold,
In a world intertwined, their humor unfolds.

Foliage Friendship

In the corner sits a fern,
Giving side-eye to the turn.
Cacti boast with prickly glee,
'Look at me! I don't need a spree!'

Philodendron flirts with grace,
'Join my leaf, don't be a waste!'
Succulents giggle in the sun,
'Who knew being green could be this fun?'

Pothos dances in the breeze,
Gossiping with chatter that pleases.
They toss their leaves with boisterous flair,
'We're the coolest plants; we swear!'

Together they thrive, despite their quirks,
A leafy crew, with fun perks.
In this green patch, laughter is shared,
Adventures grow because they dared.

Together in Bloom

In a pot that's snug and tight,
Petunias argue day and night.
'You take too much sun!' they pout,
Lilies yell, 'Let's work it out!'

The cactus rolls its pointy eyes,
'Oh, here we go with all the lies!'
While violets hum a cheerful tune,
'Let's just have fun beneath the moon!'

Daisies sprinkle joy around,
With petals soft, not a sound.
They laugh and bloom, just as they should,
Finding beauty in their good.

Together they rise, no one left out,
The world's a garden, without a doubt.
With colors bright and spirits high,
Life's a party; let's amplify!

Shades of Connection

In the shade of a crooked vine,
A chorus of leaves begins to shine.
'Why does she get all the light?'
'Is it her hair or just her height?'

A spider plant flips with style,
'When do I get my time to dial?'
The aloe laughs with its spiky glee,
'Same for me, just wait and see!'

Basil spices swirling about,
'Let's not turn this into a bout!'
With whispers of green and shades so bold,
Their bonds grow strong, their stories told.

Each sprout a spark, a jest, a trick,
Sharing warmth when the candle's wick.
Together they chant a joyous song,
In this small space, they all belong.

Growth Unison

In the window basking bright,
A jade plant claims a sunny right.
'Look at me, I'm growing tall!'
While daisies wink and tease, 'Not at all!'

The pothos trails with a sly glance,
'Let's put these folks in a dance!'
Rattlesnake plants bob with pride,
'Not a care, we'll just glide!'

Watching all from a comfy spot,
Joking and plotting, what a plot!
Life's a riot when roots entwine,
Together they flourish, so divine.

With jest and cheer, they take their place,
In this green gathering, full of grace.
Who knew that life could be this bright,
In the arms of friends, pure delight!

Moments in Leaf

In corners tucked, they giggle and sway,
Pots with secrets, brightening the day.
A cactus grins, 'I've got the spine,'
While ferns whisper, 'Life is divine.'

Sunshine spills, a watering can cheers,
Squabbles of soil, but joy appears.
Here comes the spider plant, all a-twirl,
Saying, 'I'm just trying to unfurl!'

Tiny leaves dance, in perfect sync,
Pothos trailing, with a wink and a blink.
In this leafy realm, mirth takes the lead,
A jungle of laughter, that's what they need!

Together they thrive, in humor and jest,
With little green friends, who are simply the best!
Time spent with them, oh what a delight,
In this chaotic green, the future is bright!

Hushed Growth

In the silence, a leaf starts to yawn,
Stretching wide as it greets the dawn.
Whispers of roots, beneath the ground,
'Is that a bug? I think I've found!'

The peace is shattered by a sneeze,
A playful fern, swaying with ease.
'Bless you,' the others all chime in,
'You just woke the snapdragon from within!'

A bloom peeks out, a curious sight,
Saying, 'What happened to this cozy night?'
Laughter erupts in green, tangled delight,
Even the pot's joining in on this rite!

So hush, if you can, when the plants come alive,
For in their soft giggles, true joy will thrive!

Feathered Friends and Foliage

A parakeet perched on a leafy crown,
Singing of adventures in town.
'You plants are all rooted, but I can fly,'
He flaps his wings, oh my, oh my!

The snake plant rolls its eyes so sly,
'You're just a feathered show-off, oh why?'
But all is forgiven, as sunbeams spill,
They share a space, deep on the windowsill.

A simmering jade plant lets out a sigh,
'With all this chatter, oh my, oh my!'
While the succulent tries to steal the show,
'Just blend with the soil—make it a glow!'

In this tapestry of green and a songbird's glee,
Friendship flourishes, like the sweetest decree!

The Language of Green

In the whispers of leaves, a tale unfolds,
Secrets of growth, in shades untold.
A peace lily sighs and takes a breath,
'Could you keep it down? This is my zen rest!'

The monstera grins and says with flair,
'Chill out, my friend, just breathe the air!'
With laughter and joy, they sway in delight,
Their banter blossoms, making day bright.

In the vibrant glow, they chatter and play,
Speaking in tones of green as they sway.
Each pot is a world, with stories to share,
A symphony leafy, floating in air.

So listen closely to their sweet chat,
For in every whisper, there's laughter, who'd have thought?
Plants in harmony, on this sunlit spree,
Making the world a greener jubilee!

Serenity in the Shade

In pots they sit, a leafy crew,
Arguing who gets more sunlight too,
One boasts of roots that dig so deep,
While others yawn and start to sleep.

A fussy fern demands some care,
While lazy cacti just sit there,
The succulents roll their eyes in glee,
'Not a worry in the world,' says he.

Nature's Communal Heart

The philodendron throws a party,
While orchids waltz, looking so artsy,
They talk of pests with such disdain,
'Why can't they stick to someone's grain?'

A spider plant begins to dance,
With dangling babies, take a chance,
The aloe just shakes its little head,
'Kids, this isn't what I bred!'

Green Conversations

In quiet corner, plants converse,
About the days and nights diverse,
The peace lily says, 'Let's keep it light,'
While succulents giggle, feeling bright.

The rubber tree shakes off the dust,
Saying, 'I'll thrive, in me you trust!'
The ferns all nod, they've seen it true,
But they all know who'll outgrow who!

Sheltered Silhouettes

In shadows long, they make a pact,
Together stand, no need to act,
The jade plant claims it's royalty,
While spider plants spread joy fully.

A trailing vine tells tales of thrills,
Of jumping pots and garden spills,
'Let's not forget the cat's mad rush,'
'Playful paws! They cause quite the crush!'

Harmony in the Soil

In the pot where the dirt does dwell,
Worms throw a raucous party, oh what a smell!
Cacti complain, 'Too prickly this jam!'
While violets gossip, 'Who's dating the ham?'

Sunlight pours in, everyone drinks their fill,
A fern does a jig, with the utmost of skill.
'Hey there, succulent!' the rascals shout loud,
As a rogue spider plant winks from the crowd.

But wait! Who's who in this leafy affair?
With drapes of green, they all just despair.
A pothos named Pete steals the spotlight tonight,
'This dance floor's mine, so adjust your bright light!'

Laughter erupts as they twist and they shout,
In the cozy old corner where friendships sprout.
Together they flourish, be it tall or small,
In their buzzing green world, there's room for them all.

Harmony Among the Leaves

A monstera winked, 'Did you hear the news?'
'Friendly ferns forgot to wear their shoes!'
In this jungle, who needs fancy flair?
When every leaf's laughing, it's quite the affair!

The rubber tree groaned, 'Where's my party hat?'
While spider plants tangle, and that's where it's at.
The snake plant slithered, 'I'm so cool and sleek!'
But then dripped some water, 'Oops, not my week!'

Succulents whisper, 'We're the spiky elite!'
'Yeah, but we're cute!' said each little sweet.
As air plants float, giggling high above,
In their leafy republic, there's plenty of love.

Then comes the evening, and still they delight,
Sharing tales of sunshine that sweeten their night.
In this planty soirée where all feel at ease,
They thrive in great joy, and they dance with the breeze.

Serenity in Green

In the kitchen, a basil once tried to cook,
But the garlic laughed hard, 'You're lost in a book!'
As oregano shimmied, the thyme rolled in glee,
Saying, 'Chop me nicely, and I'll make it a spree!'

Ferns danced on counters, rising to the beat,
While peas in their pods strutted tiny feet.
In a world made of soil, the joy was a lot,
Even the orchids forgot they were hot!

They'd sip on the dew that the morning had shared,
With roots intertwined, not a leaf ever scared.
When sunlight broke in, their shadows would prance,
With laughter that sparkled, they'd join in the dance.

So here in the kitchen, with laughter so bright,
Each herb and each flower is bathed in delight.
It's a garden of giggles amid culinary schemes,
Where every green friend is more than it seems.

Roots of Togetherness

Down in the dirt where the microbes reside,
The roots hold a meeting, a giggling guide.
'Let's form a parade, with our nutrient flair!'
Said the vine in the corner, while fluffing her hair.

'We'll dance under ground lights, that twinkle and glow,
Just watch out for puddles that come out of the flow!'
'Turn the compost a little!' cried out the old sage,
'If we're not careful, it's a smelly old stage!'

But laughter erupted as laughter will do,
'We're clean under here, it's the leaves that seem blue!'
With squishy delight, they grew ever bolder,
Cozy together as their roots curled and smoldered.

So here's to the roots and their silvery chats,
In the hidden green world beneath laughter and hats.
With twirls and with giggles, they quietly cheer,
In their tangled embrace, they have nothing to fear.

Unity in Foliage

In the corner sits a fern,
Doing the twist, it loves to churn.
Cacti roll their eyes in glee,
Saying, "We're not like you, oh tree!"

Succulents gossip, full of flair,
"I heard the snake plant has a scare!"
They laugh as ivy starts to creep,
"What a tangled web we keep!"

Pothos seems to stretch and yawn,
"Wake up, folks! It's nearly dawn!"
While peace lilies bloom, all white,
"Who knew we'd party through the night!"

Amidst the greenery, joy prevails,
In every pot, a tale regales.
Who knew these leaves could bring such fun?
Together, they'll shine like the sun!

The Language of Leaves

A rubber plant speaks, loud and clear,
"Hey, everyone, gather near!"
Fiddles sway like they're at a ball,
"Watch out! Here comes the spider, y'all!"

Succulents mumble, 'We're so shy,'
While the dracaena starts to fly.
"You're leafy and I'm prickly, oh dear!"
"Let's sing a song, let's give a cheer!"

Tropical vibes in a tiny space,
Every plant wears a smile on its face.
"Can you keep a secret?" they all tease,
In whispers of green that dance in the breeze.

With every leaf, a story told,
Of friendships born, both brave and bold.
In this jungle of pots, laughter erupts,
Among the green, humor interrupts!

Solace in Soil

With every scoop, there's magic found,
Beneath the roots, where dreams abound.
"Hey, don't dig too deep!" a sprout declares,
Or you'll wake the worms who have their cares!

Compost jokes, it's quite the feast,
Feeding plants, from air to beast.
"We're all in this together," they said,
While mingling in muck, where no one fled.

Dirtier hands, but brighter smiles,
Sharing secrets over gardening trials.
"You're a terrible gardener!" roared the thyme,
"But at least you're funny, so life's sublime!"

If soil could giggle, it would, for sure,
In this earthy haven, joy's the cure.
As roots entwine, a friendship grows,
In the comfy muck, laughter flows!

Harmony Among the Green

In the daylight, colors bloom,
Lively greens fill every room.
"I'm tired of sun, give me some shade!"
Said the palm with a leafy braid.

Basil frets, "Am I overcooked?"
While mint retorts, "You need a book!"
Cilantro just stirs in a pot,
"Chef, you better use what you've got!"

Foliage drapes with a carefree hue,
"Do you think we'll ever make a stew?"
"Perhaps a salad, if we could agree,"
The lettuce chuckled, "Count me free!"

So here's to laughter, roots, and green,
In a home where friends are always seen.
Amidst the chaos, balance thrives,
In this lively patch, joy survives!

A Tapestry of Growth

In the corner, a fern does sway,
Pretending it's a dancer at play.
While cactus smirks, prickly but spry,
"Try to keep up, you leafy guy!"

Pothos climbs high with mischievous glee,
Whispering secrets to the bumblebee.
"Don't mind me, I'm reaching for stars,
Just dodging the light that breaks through the bars."

Spider plant swings like it's at a fair,
With leaves that twist as if in mid-air.
"Look at me glide, I'm soaring so free,
A star of the show, don't you agree?"

Meanwhile, the jade sits, quite unbothered,
"Sheesh, why so loud? I'm calmly fathered.
In stillness, I thrive, while you all play,
You'll tire soon, and I'll win the day!"

Essence of the Earth

Caught in sunlight, green leaves prance,
As if they're auditioning for a chance.
The rubber plant puffs, "I'm the best here,
Just look at my sheen, it's abundantly clear!"

A peace lily sighs, "Oh what a tease,
Can we take a break from all the breeze?"
"Chill out," says the fern, with a whirl,
"Let's groove together, let's give it a twirl!"

Unused to the limelight, the moss stands still,
"Fun's overrated, I prefer the chill."
But the others just laugh, "You're just shy!
With vibes like yours, you could touch the sky!"

As pots rotate, some plants just pout,
"Enough of this show, let's sort it out.
We're friends in this mess, let's keep it bright,
Join hands, or leaves, for a dance tonight!"

The Dance of Foliage

In a sunny nook, a leafy jam,
With whispers of green, like a clever plan.
A tiny sprout giggles, "What's this fuss?"
"Just the epic dance of us!"

Philodendron spins with great delight,
"Watch my moves, I'm a dazzling sight!"
While orchids chime in with a swaying tune,
"Bet you can't keep up, or join our commune!"

The snake plant laughs, "You call that a dance?
My slow vibe's the real chance!"
"Don't knock it," said sage, "in the chill you find,
A rhythm that calms and soothes the mind!"

So, twirl and leap in this plant-filled ball,
The laughter and joy, they envelope us all.
From daisies to ferns, let the fun never cease,
Join this foliage fest, let chaos find peace!

Sunlight-Cast Dreams

Bathed in sunlight, the plants compete,
With a chorus of colors, oh, what a treat!
"Oh look at me shine!" said the golden pathos,
While the succulent replied, "I'm the one everyone knows!"

"I stretch to the sky, my leaves like sails,"
Said climbing ivy, spinning leafy tales.
"All this fuss, do they know it's a plot?
I'm simply here, getting all that sunhot!"

The ferns giggle, as they sway and curl,
"In this light, we're all in a whirl."
"Stay rooted, my friends," said the sterling sage,
"Joy is the game, no need to engage!"

So, in pots and pans, together we dream,
A garden of laughter, a sunlight team.
With each little petal, and each tender sprout,
It's crafting a story, of fun, there's no doubt!

Terracotta Dreams

In pots so round, with soil so rich,
The plants all chirp, a leafy pitch.
They plot and scheme from dawn to night,
Who'll get the sun? Oh, what a sight!

A cactus jests, 'I'm quite the star!'
While ferns just sigh, 'We won't go far.'
The peace lilies roll their eyes in glee,
Saying, 'Look at us, we're fancy free!'

Symphonic Sprouts

In a world of leaf and stem,
The vines all hum a sneaky hymn.
The orchids sway to a trumpet tune,
While the leafy bass just croons at noon.

Cheering suns, with rays so bright,
Conduct the jokes that ignite the night.
'Bend and twist, a dance so bold!'
Laughter erupts, as stories unfold.

Oasis of Serenity

In pots adorned with colors bright,
The plants all giggle, what a sight!
Majestic palms fan off the heat,
While succulents brag, 'We're pretty neat!'

A rubber tree sports quite the hair,
Swishing rounds like it doesn't care.
'Who needs water?' the ferns all tease,
'We'll flourish on this gentle breeze!'

Botanical Ballet

With twirls and spins, they take the floor,
A dance of greens, from leaf to spore.
The snake plant leads, with grace and flair,
While pothos drapes, without a care.

'No missteps here!' the maranta shouts,
As fronds reach high, no doubts, no pouts.
In harmony they move, so bright,
Green legs in sync, oh what a sight!

Reflections of Nature

In a pot sits Fern, feeling grand,
Stretching her leaves, waving her hand.
Cactus chuckles, with spines so sly,
'It's not easy being prickly, oh my!'

Silly Succulent, looking so thick,
Thinks he's a rock, but he's just a trick.
The Snake Plant hisses, her green is supreme,
'In this house, I'm living the dream!'

Bamboo's grooving, swaying around,
While Pothos climbs up without a sound.
Yet Little Ivy rolls her eyes wide,
'It's a jungle in here, no need to hide!'

Each plant's a character, comedy show,
Photosynthesis, but don't steal the glow!
With sunlight and laughter, they thrive every day,
In this quirky garden, they humorously play.

Botanical Symphony

In the corner, a plant with a flair,
Crooning to listeners, without any care.
The Monstera strums, on a leaf-shaped guitar,
While Traffic Light Cactus dreams of a car!

Fiddle Leaf plays, but hits the wrong note,
Yet Orchid smiles, 'It's the thought that we float!'
Together they laugh, from morning to night,
Creating a symphony, oh what a sight!

Snake Plant hums softly, a rhythmic tune,
As Pothos harmonizes, under the moon.
With every new sprout, more music takes flight,
In their leafy concert, all feels just right.

They dance in the sunlight, the plants in a row,
Throwing a bash for their leafy show.
Nature's great orchestra, comical and bright,
In this bonsai banter, pure joy ignites.

Under the Canopy

Under the big leaves, shades of delight,
Chlorophyll chuckles at morning's first light.
Each stem tells a story, each leaf has its say,
As critters parade, the plants join the play.

Spider Plant spins webs of silly tales,
While Rubber Tree giggles, with big, shiny scales.
Together they whisper, 'What fun it can be,
To live in a jungle, with total esprit!'

A little Bonsai, so tiny and spry,
Wishes for wings, to soar through the sky.
While Peace Lily sighs, 'I'm stuck in this place,
But hey, there's still light and smiles to embrace!'

With shades of green laughing, and colors so bright,
Their banter fills air, a humorous sight.
Under the canopy, life swings with delight,
In this potbound paradise, all feels just right.

Gentle Leaves

Gentle leaves dance, in the soft summer breeze,
Making up stories, with giggles and tease.
A tiny plant whispers, 'Oh look at me shine!'
While tall Zamioculcas leans, feeling divine!

Zesty little Aloe, with juice oh so sweet,
Claims he's a healer, can't be beat!
While the Pilea smiles, her coins on display,
'I'm rich with good vibes, that's how I play!'

Calathea twirls, patterns aglow,
'Watch my moves, I'm the star of the show!'
While droopy Fern murmurs, with a frown on her face,
'Please stop the spinning; give me some space!'

With whispers and giggles that fill up the air,
In this vibrant world, there's laughter to share.
Each leaf is a dreamer, full of surprise,
In this garden of joy, where happiness lies.

Soothing Hearts

In pots of laughter, with chirps and gleams,
The plants smile softly, fulfilling their dreams.
Monsteras tease, with their big, leafy grin,
'We keep it cheerful—now let the fun begin!'

Tiny Basil, a chef's best friend,
Jokes about dinner, it's all just pretend.
While Lavender winks, with a calming embrace,
'If life gets too loud, I'll give it some grace!'

Peace Plant whispers, 'Let's take it slow,'
Yoga with Fern, as they stretch to grow.
With roots intertwined, their hearts full of cheer,
They brighten each moment, from far and near.

In a quirky dance, they make life a part,
Together they flourish, soothing each heart.
In this pot of giggles, love blooms and spins,
With every green leaf, a new joy begins!

Clusters of Comfort

In pots they sit, gossiping with glee,
Leaves bending low, sipping their tea.
Cacti with sass, while ferns softly sway,
Bantering blooms, just a usual day.

The spider plant's swing, it's a sight to behold,
While succulents giggle, their stories retold.
Is that a new leaf on that one in the back?
Oh please, let's toast with this glass of flax snack!

Intertwined Life

In a sunbeam's dance, they twist and they twirl,
A thriller of colors, in a leafy swirl.
Vines play hopscotch, through pots they leap,
With whispers and chuckles, secrets they keep.

The rubber tree's dreams, oh how vast they grow,
While little ferns pout, "We need more to show!"
The orchids roll eyes, "Oh, spare us the fuss!"
As rubber and ivy join in the trust!

Nature's Collective Breath

A party of greens, under dust motes they dance,
Exchanging sweet secrets, as if by chance.
A pothos floats by, with a winking delight,
While the bamboo nods slow—he's just feeling light.

The fiddle leaf fig strums a tune with its leaves,
And the peace lily giggles—oh, what a tease!
With laughter of branches, they share every tale,
Rooted in joy, they'll never turn pale!

The Quiet Symphony

A symphony whispers with leaves soft and bright,
Each plant in its pot, plays its role just right.
With a jingle and jiggle, the herbs smell divine,
While the ferns shake their fronds in a choreographed line.

The cactus plays drums, with a poky good cheer,
While violets bloom sweetly, "We love it in here!"
Though the lamp looks on, casting shadows and light,
Together they thrive, in their leafy delight.

Foliage's Sweet Soliloquy

With leaves that wiggle and sway,
They dance in their pots all day.
Whispers of care with no fuss,
They giggle in green, what a plus!

When sunlight peeks through the blinds,
A leafy gossip softly unwinds.
"Did you hear what the fern just said?"
"Oh please, it's just a plant in bed!"

Each morning brings fresh delight,
As they chat about last night's light.
But watch out for that sneaky vine,
Its curls are plotting, oh so fine!

In this leafy place where we dwell,
There's joy in every petal's swell.
A chorus of greens, all in glee,
To their own tune, they sway carefree!

Secretive Green Gatherings

In the corner, the cactus is shy,
But it's got stories that could make you cry.
"Why's everyone looking so prim?"
"Oh, that's just the succulents' whim!"

The orchids whisper with flair,
"Shh! Let's not disturb the creepy air!"
They hold their meetings on the sly,
With petals and leaves that never lie.

Ferns throw a party, so lush and grand,
Bringing twists of vines, a wild band.
"Just don't let the cat come near,"
Or it's an instant plant-astrophe here!

Moss collects tales like nature's book,
Every secret is worth a look.
They giggle and shake in their earthy bed,
In this thriving green league, never misled!

Echoes of Photosynthesis

In the warmth of sun's embrace,
They hold their breath, a leafy race.
Photosynthesis, what a spree,
Come join the fun, just wait and see!

The leafy choir sings in delight,
Producing smiles with all their might.
"Hey there, buddy, how's your chlorophyll?"
"Great! But let me share this grass will!"

With sunlight streaming, they stretch and yawn,
A leafy comedy breaks every dawn.
"I swear I saw that pothos slink,
Was it reaching for water, or just a drink?"

So let's raise a leaf to this green brigade,
In their quirky ways, joy is made.
With jokes in the shade and bright debates,
They're the best plant pals, oh how fate waits!

In the Shade of Togetherness

Nestled close, a leafy crew,
Sharing sunlight, rain, and dew.
"Do you think we'll grow too wide?"
"Only if the sun's our guide!"

In this cozy, verdant spot,
No plant shall feel that they're forgot.
With roots that tangle, laughter swells,
"Watch your leaves, they're just like spells!"

Fiddling fiddle-leaf's got a tune,
Whistling softly to the morning's rune.
"I can't help it, the light's too bright,"
And away they sway, what a sight!

Side by side in their leafy home,
In shadows and sunshine, they brightly roam.
A friendship forged in soil and care,
In their thriving patch, there's love to share!

The Sanctuary of Growth

In a pot sat a cactus so prickly and sly,
He told the pansies, "Oh, don't be shy!"
With a wiggle and giggle, they danced in the sun,
A floral fiesta—oh, what fun!

The fern wore a hat, made of silk and lace,
While the ivy whispered secrets from its green space.
"Who knew roots had rhythm, and stems could sway?"
They laughed all afternoon, 'til the end of the day.

A lonely old pot had a large leafy dream,
To host all the plants for a wild, leafy theme.
They'd drink up their water and sway with delight,
As they shimmied and shook in the pale moonlight!

At dusk they shared stories, of sunlight and rain,
Each plant had a tale, with a quirky refrain.
"So let's grow together, with humor and glee!"
And that's how they thrived, in their sanctuary!

Gentle Roots

In the corner, a pothos climbed so high,
He winked at the ficus, "What's the rush? Oh my!"
The snake plant chuckled, "Relax and unwind,
We've got all the time, and sunshine to find."

Beneath the table, the soil had a chat,
With worms telling jokes, it was quite a spat!
"Why don't we ever get lost in the dirt?"
"Because our roots keep us grounded, covered, and curt!"

The orchid, so posh, sported petals like lace,
"Living in this pot is a beautiful grace!"
But the spider plant scoffed, with a wink of its leaf,
"You know, we're all gorgeous, but I'm the chief!"

With laughter and cheer, they intertwined,
Those gentle roots had a love well-defined.
In their quirky little world, all species unite,
Blooming and blooming, on each sunny night!

Flora's Melody

The daisies danced in a perfect line,
While the bromeliad sang, 'Isn't life divine?'
"Watch out for the car, it's barking a tune!"
They swayed to the rhythm of a very strange June!

The rubber plant joked, "I could bounce off the wall!"
While the lavender twirled, with a fragrant sprawl.
"Are you in a pot or just having a blast?"
"Both!" chimed the soil—"We're weeding the past!"

A melody echoed from leaves far and wide,
A chorus of greenery, all side by side.
"Let's celebrate life, with a sprinkle of spice!"
And the plants danced together, oh how they were nice!

So here's to the laughter, the joy, and the play,
In flora's grand symphony, brightening the day.
With roots intertwined, and laughter that rang,
Life's never too dull, when the plants like to hang!

Nature's Chorus

In the morning light, the sun made its way,
Tickling the leaves, waking them for play.
The succulent sighed, "Life's just a breeze,
Especially with friends, let's spread joy with ease!"

The begonias blushed, oh so brightly,
While the geraniums giggled—"Not too sprightly!"
They played hide and seek, behind foliage tall,
And the herb pot chimed in, "I'll grow through it all!"

The peace lily chimed in, with calm and with flair,
"Let's nurture our laughter, and breathe in the air!"
"I'm a bit of a flirt," joked the tongue plant with glee,
"I make all the bees buzz, come and dance near me!"

So with tides of humor, and roots of delight,
In nature's chorus, everything felt right.
Together they thrived, through sunshine and storm,
Creating a garden, a cozy, fun form!

www.ingramcontent.com/pod-product-compliance
Lightning Source LLC
Chambersburg PA
CBHW070321120526
44590CB00017B/2775